GW00362951

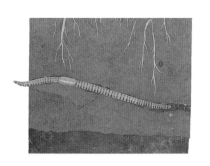

SOIL

A WORM'S EYE VIEW

by

PENELOPE
HOBHOUSE

JOHN BROWN PUBLISHING

FOREWORD

Most gardening techniques are very simple and can be discovered by using common sense and imagination. Getting the soil right is the first priority. Good, well-prepared tilth with plenty of earthworms is obviously going to give plants a good start. If the worms are happy plants will probably thrive. Planting correctly is another essential. This includes choosing plants with well-developed root systems, and avoiding those which have been badly grown or are pot-bound. Each plant or group of plants must have the right soil and climatic conditions. It is no use planting acid-loving plants in alkaline soil or planting the moisture lovers where they will dry out.

Established woody plants need pruning and training, often on an annual basis, and most soft-stemmed perennials need dividing in order to maintain their vigour. The most fun in gardening comes from making new plants from old; propagating from cuttings and growing new plants or replacements from seed.

Gardening carefully and thoughtfully brings its own rewards. The pleasure of watching things grow, waiting patiently, not hurrying results, that is the best way to gain experience. Like the garden itself, gardening know-how grows with time.

Getting the soil in good heart is of primary importance if, over the years, a garden is to develop satisfactorily. As a garden designer, I have become more and more interested in soil management, though I have to admit my knowledge has not developed in a scientific way. I need down-to-earth strategies that work for all the different types of soil I encounter, strategies that are adaptable to each of the many situations I meet in my clients' gardens. Designing gardens in many different areas of the world, I have had to cope with just about every possible variant in soil. Getting the soil to a standard suitable for planting is sometimes extremely demanding, but adequate preparation is a vital element in ensuring success for a design.

The most difficult soil I have encountered so far is the alkaline clay found in parts of Texas. This clay is heavy, sticky and almost impossible to work: it has poor drainage, inadequate aeration and quite limited nutrient retention. In addition, this most exacting of soils is found in a region where the climate makes gardening arduous no matter what the type of soil. Temperatures can swing in a day from a blistering 42° Centigrade (108° Fahrenheit) to below freezing when cold northerly winds sweep down from the Canadian plains. We had the most success when we used native plants from this region.

Few soils will prove as formidable to improve. Yet in general challenging soil conditions are not rare. The most common of serious problems I encounter is topsoil compacted by heavy machinery used in construction. To improve such solid and unworkable soil it is necessary to cultivate it to as great a depth as possible, incorporating organic matter that keeps 'open' the newly created spaces made by digging. This can take many weeks of hard work in preparation and the most difficult soil types needing continual amendments with grit and organic mulches.

Sometimes it may be better to replace the difficult, unworkable soil with some new topsoil after breaking up and improving the texture of the sub-stratas. Obtaining new topsoil is not easy. Suppliers are generally geared towards supplying the garden trade and will only deliver if you want a considerable amount of new topsoil.

What is topsoil? The old definition of topsoil as the original surface layer of grass or cultivated land (the coveted loam described later) is seldom realistic, although it is still possible in country areas to find suppliers of topsoil created from rotting turf with pebbles and stones screened out. Near my home in Dorset I can now get screened soil from reputable sources. Usually the soil comes from contractors excavating for new housing and one keeps one's eyes open for new building developments in areas of good, friable (workable) soil. However, it may be necessary to accept a second best, using 'soil' composed of sub-soil with a mineral base, enhanced by organic matter and nutrients.

FRIABLE SOIL - a workable tilth with a good texture - is a precious garden commodity. Unfortunately most soils need amendment before achieving the right texture. Adequate soil preparation is essential for plants and for earthworms.

11

Most gardeners will best solve their soil problems through improving what they have. I find when designing gardens that good, workable soil seldom exists on site - it almost always has to be 'made'. Consider how hard your soil has to work for you. It is the soil that provides plants with essential nutrients and with moisture at their roots. It is soil that houses those roots and keeps them protected from the extremes of climate changes. Good soil has the following qualities. It retains nutrients so roots can be nourished. It has a good texture so roots can pass through the soil with ease yet establish a firm foundation for the plant. It neither drains too quickly nor holds water too long so adequate drainage enables roots to obtain sufficient moisture without becoming waterlogged. It warms up in early spring and cools slowly through autumn to provide a long growing season.

How do you make good soil? Central to my approach when planning soil improvements and changes is to try to think like an earthworm and to provide the sort of soil in which they would thrive.

THINK LIKE A WORM

The raw material of soil comes from the weathering of rocks into mixtures of different particle sizes. The soil itself is a complex combination of inert minerals, chemicals and organic materials - the nutrients. It is also colonised by millions of microscopic organisms that make the vital nutrients available to the roots of the plants. Earthworms are the most important soil organisms; their digestive tracts are literally fertiliser

factories aerating the soil, and making channels for roots and for moisture. Apparently, there should be at least ten earthworms per cubic foot (0.03 cubic metres) of soil. So as one assesses the quality of soil, think like a worm.

REALLY GOOD GARDEN SOIL should have at least ten earthworms per cubic foot. Neutral, or optimum, pH is 6.5 but most plants will tolerate a range between 5.5 and 7.5. Topsoil should be dug over to at least two spits or spade heads deep before planting. After that do not dig the beds but add a generous layer of organic mulch twice a year, in the autumn and spring, to maintain the soil.

THE SOIL'S pH RANGE

Earthworms are unable to survive in very acid soils (below a pH of 4.5). The pH of soil measures its acidity or alkalinity which affects the availability of plant nutrients. You can buy kits for measuring your pH range that are straightforward to use. The higher the pH reading, the higher the alkaline content of the soil. The pH range for good plant growth lies between 5.5 pH and 7.5 pH with 6.5 pH as the optimum. Most plants are reasonably tolerant of this range but gardeners quickly learn which plants, particularly ericaceous varieties, such as azaleas and rhododendrons, will not thrive in a soil with high pH (calcifuge). Others, such as roses and viburnums, peonies and sweet peas, prefer alkaline conditions (calcicole) thriving in a pH between 6.5 and 7.5, and almost all vegetables benefit from a lime dressing if the pH is below 6.

When I am designing in a new area, I only send soil away for a complete analysis if I suspect a serious mineral deficiency, usually indicated with yellowing or blotchy leaves. I will take pH readings of topsoil from various parts of a garden. These readings may well vary depending on how intensively each area has been cultivated. You can make a good educated guess about the soil type and likely pH by observing plants in the immediate district surrounding a garden. Look at native trees and shrubs, as well as flourishing garden plants. I never advise trying to lower a pH in order to grow acid-loving plants in alkaline conditions; lime from surrounding soil will leach into the amended soil after a short period. Instead, grow them in containers of specially prepared ericaceous soil. On the other hand, lime can be added to an acid soil with low pH to increase alkalinity for vegetable growing and for the real lime-lovers (calcicoles).

ESSENTIAL NUTRIENTS

In order to thrive, plants require three primary nutrients: Nitrogen (N), Phosphorus (P) and Potassium (K). Magnesium, Calcium and Sulphur are important secondary nutrients and there are further essential trace elements, but these are needed only in very small quantities. Nitrogen stimulates growth and gives plant leaves their rich green colour. Too much Nitrogen can lead to too rapid growth at the expense of flowers. Phosphorus stimulates the growth of seedlings, and in particular the fibrous root system. Traditionally Potassium promotes flowers and fruit and a lack of Potassium will result in poor flowers and fruit that may drop off the branch before maturing.

Nutrients are lost to the soil by leaching; that is when excess water carries away the minerals. Nutrients are also, of course, lost by uptake into vegetation and need constant replacement. This can be done through applying mulch such as decayed leaves, or other organic matter, to the area around plants. You can also feed with nutrients to assist particular plants, using artificial fertilisers which give a quick boost, especially in spring. Whether you use organic or chemical fertilisers and feeds, you are advised to follow the manufacturers' recommenda-

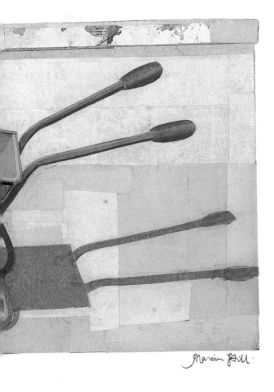

Marcin Grill

tions. General purpose fertilisers contain Nitrogen, Phosphorous and Potassium – the three basic nutrients – as well as other essential minerals. Some general fertilisers come recommended for particular types of plants – such as flowers or vegetables. All these general feeds will assist the soil and help plant growth. There is a constant debate about the use of chemicals as opposed to organic fertilisers (similarly the debate continues about weed and pest killers) and the decision has to be left to the individual gardener. If you feel your soil is not rich enough to support your plants, it is a good idea to supplement nutrients with a general feed around root areas. There are also many fertilisers designed for specific plants – particularly roses. These feeds have been formulated to give maximum growth for these specific plants. Again, as you get to know both your soil and your plants, you will be the best judge as to whether you need to feed them. It is certainly recommended after pruning or moving a plants's position, when a plant needs extra help.

However, it is important to remember that such fertilisers are no substitute for reconditioning and improving your soil with a thorough layer of mulch or compost applied twice a year. If the soil is not in good condition, the plants cannot take up the artificial nutrients.

Mulching creates humus and improves the plants possibilities of taking up nutrients. Equally, if not more important, since the richness of the soil is directly linked to it, is the texture and type of the soil. The two things are inextricably connected and nothing will improve texture more than regular mulching. It is important to understand the type of soil that you are working with.

LOAM: THE IDEAL SOIL

The soil a mole throws up in its excavations is the ideal: loam. However irritating a mole's hills on a lawn, the consistency and rich colour of the earth it has excavated is a fine indicator of how good soil can be. Scientifically described as a mixture of large and small particles, loam is the very best possible

MOLES DIG, scratch and tunnel in the soil to produce a fine, 'worked' loam, a mixture of large and small particles that runs easily through your fingers, perfect for planting.

soil type for the gardener, with an optimum combination of properties. Good drainage, moisture retention and nutrient-holding capacity are all essential. Loam warms up relatively quickly in spring and retains heat through the autumn, giving a good growing season. Worms are sublimely happy in it. This perfect type of loam soil is what you would find in an old, well-worked kitchen garden. Sadly, you are more likely to have a less than perfect soil.

CLAY: HEAVY SOIL

Clay soil has the smallest particles of all soil-types; it is self-binding and becomes easily waterlogged in winter or compacted in summer. Squeezed between finger and thumb it will form a sticky ball. In compacted clay there are few earthworms. Heavy clay can be rich in nutrients and highly fertile, though is often so compacted that plants have difficulty in developing adequate root systems. Roots simply cannot push their way through such heavily compacted soil. Clay takes time to heat up after the winter but equally it holds the heat of summer longer than lighter soils so gives a growing season that stretches through the autumn months.

SAND: LIGHT SOIL

At the opposite extreme is a light sandy soil with large soil particles. Although nearly always easy to work, sandy soils are fast draining and drought-prone, needing irrigation and then frequent applications of organic matter to help them retain nutrients, which wash away easily. Worms, sensitive to drought, do not thrive in light sandy soils. Light soils gain heat early in the spring, but lose it with similar speed as temperatures drop in autumn, so their growing season can be relatively short.

SILT: A GOOD MIDDLE SOIL

Silt is a soil that consists of particles somewhere between clay and sand in size. Silt soils tend to compact easily but are generally water-retentive and usually fertile.

DEALING WITH BAD SOILS

Both extremes of heavy clay and light sand, and the many variations of silts between, can be improved. Whatever your soil, digging in organic matter will assist the texture and workability and help the essential micro-organisms to thrive. In heavy clay soil, the addition of organic compost as well as gravel or grit helps particles to aggregate into larger workable 'crumbs' and allows earthworms free travel. In lighter, sandy soils, organic matter helps reduce drainage and bind the large particles while preventing loss of nutrients through rapid leaching.

I firmly believe the best starting point for improving texture is double digging the soil to a depth of almost two 'spits', or two depths of the spade head. Rotovation, using a mechanical rotovator, especially on clay soils, is not always advisable. It leads to the formation of a hard pan at a depth directly below where the rotovator reaches. This pan will inhibit root growth after the first few seasons and water will gather there rather than draining away. Similarly, if you dig over a flowerbed to a depth of only one spade head, the soil below can remain compacted and roots cannot break through the hard layer.

Except on very difficult clays, flowerbeds need only be given a really thorough double digging once, adding organic matter and gravel as the digging proceeds. In future years, seasonal mulching should keep up the humus content and augment nutrients. In my own garden, however, we did prepare the soil with a thorough double-digging three or four times.

When I moved to the Marshwood Vale in Dorset in 1994, the very heavy clay proved to be the most difficult soil I had encountered, outside of Texas. The garden here at Bettiscomb serves as a useful example of how to improve soil texture and ensure future workability. Drainage was the first essential in my inner walled garden and before starting to improve the soil I created a network of drains. In order to check if drainage is adequate, dig holes 60-90 cm (2-3 ft) deep and fill them with water. If the water does not drain away in a few hours you need to create a drainage system or only grow plants which are tolerant of   water-logged conditions in winter. Willows and alders are an obvious example and hornbeam is much more tolerant than beech. These heavy clays are usually wet in winter but dry in summer – sometimes to cement-like hardness in summer, so are not necessarily suitable for moisture-loving bog plants which, tolerant of being wet in winter, also need moisture through the growing season. The wet clay, inhospitable to many perennials that

31

dislike having water round their crowns in winter, may be highly suitable for annuals which are only placed in the garden as the soil dries out at the end of May. A simple drainage system of herringbone pattern done with gravel or plastic pipes feeds into a main channel which empties into a sump outside the garden area. A slight fall, about 1:40, is necessary and on level ground can be achieved by adjusting the depth of drains. It is probably worth calling in a professional who will use modern materials.

After five years of hard work, the soil in my garden is starting to 'make it', but the heavy, waterlogged clay needs constant improvement and lightening. Rock-hard like cement in summer with widening cracks in a period of drought, sticky and plastic in winter, the soil needs grit, gypsum, and organic

Marion Hill

matter to make it workable. Even after five years try-ing to avoid compaction, we can still only work dur-ing the brief spring and autumn windows, when con-ditions are favourable. Endless on-going amendment is essential and we add grit with each plant. Planting bulbs is still a nightmare and the early spring anemones, muscari and chionodoxas, are only just beginning to spread.

Fortunately, with the texture improved, the soil has proved to be very fertile - impossibly so for any attempts at creating a flowering meadow but great for suitable shrubs, roses and tough perennials.

To eradicate troublesome weeds we allowed flowerbeds to lie empty for a whole season, during which time weeds were dug out or destroyed with chemicals. Japanese knotweed, mare's tail and bindweed all throve in the poor undrained sticky clay. We still have some residual mare's tail but as this prefers poor conditions it gets weaker each season; now that the soil is loosened and friable I can pull it out by hand. Knotweed and bind weed have been destroyed by glycosphate which only affects the plants which it touches and does not leach into neighbouring areas.

After the initial double-diggings, incorporating mushroom compost and gravel, we have concentrated on covering any bare earth with an organic mulch to a depth of 5-8cm (2-3in). We do this twice annually, once in the autumn and again in the spring to early summer. We now have our own compost and supplement this with extra mushroom compost which contains gypsum (hydrated calcium sulphate)

THE IDEAL WAY to make compost for mulching is to prepare three compartments, or bays, lined with wood or narrow-gauge wire netting. One is for the initial storage of organic waste, the next for turning it into, and the third for final storage until the compost is used.

a substance that does not make the soil more alkaline and helps as a clay-breaker.

COMPOST

We make our compost quite casually, assuming on waiting a year for the compost of garden greens (including some grass mowings), leaves and cow-manure to mature. We make this in wire cages 3 x 4m (10 x 13ft) and turn it once or twice during the early stages. You can speed this process up by using a proven compost activator.

Making your own compost bin is going to benefit your garden. The ideal manageable size is 120cm tall x 120cm wide by 120cm deep (4ft x 4ft x 4ft), to allow for the right balance of heat and air circulation. For best results, place your bin on bare soil in a warm, though open, site. Good ingredients include egg shells, nettle tops, young growth of annual weeds, vegetable peelings, bedding from vegetarian pets such as rabbits and gerbils, pure wool jumpers, water (if the compost is dry), chicken and pigeon manure, farmyard and horse manure. Good compost activators include grass mowings, nettles, comfrey, diluted human urine, fresh manure, commercial activators available from garden centres. Always avoid adding dog and cat faeces or litter, coal ash, meat or fish scraps.

MULCH

Any organic mulch adds humus to the soil as it rots down and if you are unable to provide enough of your own compost, and few are, there are many other organic mulches including: straw, sawdust, bark (although I do not like its municipal look nor the way it depletes the nitrogen in the soil); and coir (though the latter dries out easily). Gravel is an attractive mulch, ideal for plants, providing natural drainage around their crowns and roots, to protect them in freezing periods. More plants die from water freezing around their roots than from actual cold. Gravel also provides a moisture-retentive layer in summer during drought.

Leaf mould is highly desirable, especially if you can make your own from well-rotted beech leaves.

SPREAD MULCH carefully around the plants to a depth of about 15 cm (6 in) avoiding plant crowns and young stems.

41

Some leaves such as those of oak and plane trees take a long time to decompose and need a separate compost cage to allow for ageing.

Well-rotted manures can work well and I dig well-rotted farmyard manure into vegetable beds. However, I seldom use cow or horse manure as mulch without storing it for at least a year. It is often full of weed seeds that germinate once it is spread.

In commercial horticulture layers of an inorganic mulch such as black plastic will raise soil temperatures and suppress weed germination but unless covered are too unsightly for a private garden. I do use a membrane, which allows water through it, in my vegetable area and cover it with an attractive layer of workmanlike bark.

Organic mulches help retain moisture and nutrients, improve the soil texture, reduce risk of compaction and disease, and by increasing the humus content encourage the plants to make strong root systems. Mulches act as a cosmetic - particularly useful in a new garden - and regulate soil temperature by providing insulation. Mulch also suppresses weeds and prevents weed seed germination. Mulch in autumn to help hold the heat in the soil; mulch in spring or early summer, after the soil has warmed up but before the moisture has evaporated, and you not only suppress weeds but also prevent the soil drying out. Never mulch during a drought without giving the soil a good soaking first as the covering layer will prevent any rain shower from penetrating. Mulches can ideally be about 15cm (6in) thick but should not be placed over the crown of perennials and neither should it touch the stems or bark of newly-planted woody shrubs.

Here at Bettiscombe we never make enough of our own compost to mulch the whole garden and I continue to buy-in waste mushroom compost which I stockpile for future use. I operate a sort of dual system that ensures that most areas of soil are covered with mulch most of the time. I make certain that there are spaces of bare soil so that the seeds of alchemilla, aquilegias, eryngiums, valerian, violas, hellebores, sweet rocket, euphorbias, and several other prolific seeders that set the style of my garden, can germinate. For any new garden these volunteer seedlings are an essential ingredient.

SALVIA sclarea turkestanica is a possible self-seeding plant.

Marian Hill

ACKNOWLEDGEMENTS

ILLUSTRATIONS by Marian Hill
DESIGNED by Roger Walton
PRODUCTION by Imago Publishing Ltd

Photograph of Penelope Hobhouse by Charles Hopkinson

First published in Great Britain by John Brown Publishing Ltd,
The New Boathouse, 136-142 Bramley Road, London
W10 6SR

ISBN 1-902212-266

Printed and bound in China for Imago

GARDENS
ILLUSTRATED

Take out a SPECIAL OFFER subscription to the world's leading gardening magazine. Only £29.50 for 10 issues, a saving of 15%.

I would like to take out a subscription to GARDENS ILLUSTRATED

☐ 1 year (10 issues): £29.50 UK; £45.00 Europe, £60.00 rest of world

☐ 2 years (20 issues): £58.00 UK; £89.00 Europe, £110.00 rest of world

☐ I enclose a cheque payable to John Brown Publishing (sterling cheques only)

for £ _____

I would like to pay by credit/debit card. Please charge my:

☐ VISA   ☐ MASTERCARD   ☐ AMEX   ☐ EUROCARD

☐ CONNECT   ☐ SWITCH: issue no./start date ☐☐☐

Card Number ☐☐☐☐ ☐☐☐☐ ☐☐☐☐ ☐☐☐☐

Expiry Date ☐☐☐☐

Signature _____ Date _____

Name _____

Address _____

_____ Postcode _____

Telephone _____ Email _____

Send this form to: GARDENS ILLUSTRATED, SUBSCRIPTIONS, FREEPOST (SWB837), BRISTOL BS32 0ZZ   (No stamp needed in the UK). Or phone 01454 618 905.

Money back guarantee: you may cancel your subscription at any time if not completely satisfied and receive a refund on all unmailed issues. GARDENS ILLUSTRATED is published by John Brown Publishing Ltd, The New Boathouse, 136-142 Bramley Road, London W10 6SR

CUT ALONG HERE